THE ANIMALS OF ASIA

ASIAN DOLPHINS AND OTHER MARINE MAMMALS

WILLOW CLARK

PowerKiDS press

New York

Published in 2013 by The Rosen Publishing Group, Inc.
29 East 21st Street, New York, NY 10010

Copyright © 2013 by The Rosen Publishing Group, Inc.

All rights reserved. No part of this book may be reproduced in any form without permission in writing from the publisher, except by a reviewer.

First Edition

Editor: Joanne Randolph
Book Design: Ashley Drago
Layout Design: Julio Gil

Photo Credits: Cover Gerard Soury/Oxford Scientific/Getty Images; p. 4 © Juniors Bildarchiv/age fotostock; p. 5 © www.iStockphoto.com/Dejan Sarman; p. 7 AleksandrN/Shutterstock.com; p. 8 Willyam Bradberry/Shutterstock.com; p. Krzysztof Odziomek/Shutterstock.com; p. 10 Photo Researchers/Getty Images; p. 11 Sokolov Elexey/Shutterstock.com; p. 12 Gerard Soury/Peter Arnold/Getty Images; p. 13 Tang Chhin Sothy/AFP/Getty Images; p. 14 Dorling Kindersley RF/Thinkstock.com; p. 15 © David Sellwood/age fotostock; p. 16 Dray van Beeck/Shutterstock.com; p. 17 (top) Sami Sarkis/Photographer's Choice/Getty Images; p. 17 (bottom) Doug Perrine/Peter Arnold/Getty Images; p. 18 withGod/Shutterstock.com; p. 19 (left) Bruno Morandi/The Image Bank/Getty Images; p. 19 (right) Planet Observer/Universal Image Group/Getty Images; p. 20 China Photos/Stringer/Getty Images; p. 21 © Masa Ushioda/age fotostock; p. 22 Mark Carwardine/Peter Arnold/Getty Images.

Library of Congress Cataloging-in-Publication Data

Clark, Willow.
Asian dolphins and other marine mammals / by Willow Clark. — 1st ed.
p. cm. — (The animals of Asia)
Includes index.
ISBN 978-1-4488-7419-4 (library binding) — ISBN 978-1-4488-7492-7 (pbk.) —
 ISBN 978-1-4488-7566-5 (6-pack)
1. Dolphins—Asia—Juvenile literature. 2. Marine mammals—Asia—Juvenile literature. I. Title.
QL737.C432C547 2013
599.53—dc23

2012004241

Manufactured in China

CPSIA Compliance Information: Batch #WKTS12PK: For Further Information contact Rosen Publishing, New York, New York at 1-800-237-9932

CONTENTS

THE WATERS OF ASIA 4
WHAT ARE MARINE MAMMALS? 6
WHERE IN THE WORLD? 8
FRESHWATER OR SALTWATER? 10
IRRAWADDY DOLPHIN 12
INDO-PACIFIC HUMPBACKED DOLPHIN ... 14
DUGONG 16
LAKE BAIKAL SEAL 18
FINLESS PORPOISE 20
MARINE MAMMALS IN DANGER 22
GLOSSARY 23
INDEX 24
WEBSITES 24

THE WATERS OF ASIA

The oceans and rivers throughout Asia are filled with wildlife. Some of its most fascinating animals are **marine** mammals, such as dolphins. Some of these animals live in freshwater. Others live in salt water. There are even animals that live in somewhat salty, or **brackish**, waters. Brackish

The Indo-Pacific humpbacked dolphin is one of Asia's marine mammals. This dolphin lives in the Indian and Pacific Oceans.

Dugongs live in the waters of the Indian Ocean, Pacific Ocean, and the Red Sea. Related to manatees, they spend a lot of time eating underwater grasses and plants.

water is often found in places where freshwater and salt water mix.

Many of these marine mammals, such as the Irrawaddy dolphin, are in trouble. Their numbers are falling due to pollution and the damming of rivers. They also get caught in nets meant for other animals. This book will introduce you to some of these amazing Asian animals.

WHAT ARE MARINE MAMMALS?

Marine mammals such as dolphins, dugongs, and seals live in the ocean **biome**. They are very different from fish, though. Unlike fish, mammals are warm-blooded. This means that they make their own body heat. Mammals also **nurse** their young with milk from their bodies.

WHERE MARINE MAMMALS LIVE

This map shows where several different kinds of Asian marine mammals can be found. ▼

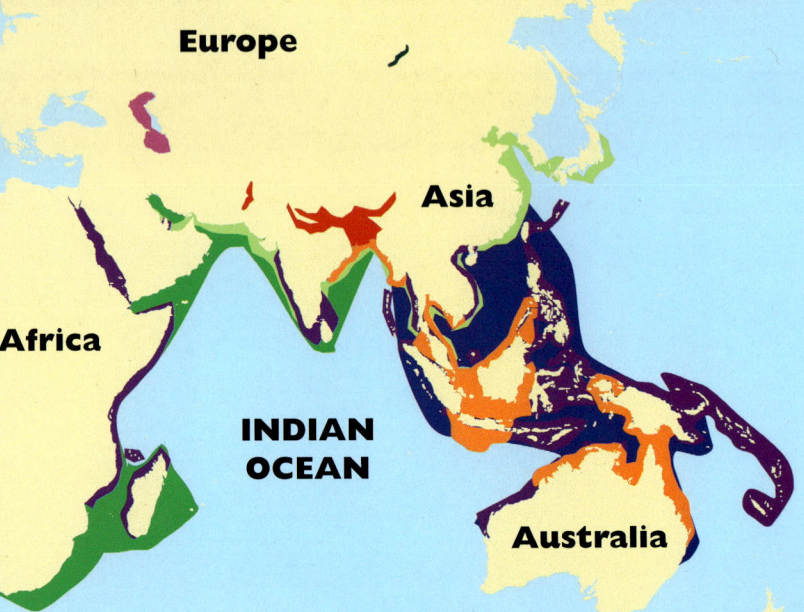

KEY
- Dugong range
- Irrawaddy dolphin range
- Indo-Pacific humpbacked dolphin range
- Indian humpbacked dolphin range
- South Asian river dolphin range
- Lake Baikal seal range
- Caspian Sea seal range
- Finless porpoise range

▲ Many marine mammals have fur like these seals that live in the White Sea, in Russia, do.

Most marine mammals have fur or hair on their bodies, as land mammals do. Lake Baikal and Caspian Sea seals have fur that is easy to see. Dugongs have fine hairs on their skin. Dolphins are nearly hairless. Some young dolphins have hair around their snouts when they are born, which they later lose.

WHERE IN THE WORLD?

Asia's marine mammals are found in its rivers and **estuaries** as well as in its oceans and seas. The South Asian river dolphin is a freshwater dolphin. It lives in the Ganges and Indus Rivers in India, Nepal, Pakistan, and Bangladesh. These dolphins are **endangered** due to hunting, pollution, damming of rivers in their habitat, and getting caught in fishing nets.

This dugong lives in the Red Sea. It uses its whiskers like feelers to help it find sea grasses to eat.

These dolphins hunt for fish in the Red Sea. Some dolphins, such as spinner and bottlenose dolphins, live in waters near Asia but also live near other continents, too.

Dugongs live in the warm, coastal waters of the Red Sea, Indian Ocean, and the Pacific Ocean. Laws in many parts of their range protect these **vulnerable** ocean mammals.

Lake Baikal and the Caspian Sea are bodies of water within the Asian continent. Seals live in both of these bodies of water.

FRESHWATER OR SALTWATER?

Dolphins, whales, and porpoises all belong to the same scientific order, or grouping, called Cetacea. The animals in this order are called cetaceans. Most of them live in the ocean. There are three living **species** of freshwater dolphins, though.

Indo-Pacific humpbacked dolphins like warm, shallow ocean water best and sometimes hunt in the brackish water of estuaries and mangrove swamps.

▲ *Bottlenose dolphins are some of the best-known dolphins in the world. These dolphins live in salty ocean water.*

Freshwater dolphins have a few **adaptations** that set them apart from marine dolphins. Freshwater dolphins generally have snouts that are about four times longer than those of marine dolphins. These snouts help them find fish along riverbanks. Freshwater dolphins also have smaller eyes and poorer eyesight than marine dolphins. River water is often muddy, so good eyesight would not help these dolphins much! They count on **echolocation** to find food, instead.

IRRAWADDY DOLPHIN

The Irrawaddy dolphin is not a true river dolphin. Irrawaddy dolphins are adapted to live in different tropical aquatic environments. They are named for the Irrawaddy River, in Myanmar, one of the freshwater rivers in which they live. They are also

There are only about 85 Irrawaddy dolphins left in the Mekong River.

Some groups of Irrawaddy dolphins are always in freshwater. Two of these freshwater groups are the dolphins in Chilka Lake, in India, and Songhkla Lake, in Thailand.

found in the brackish estuaries and coastal waters of the Indian Ocean and Pacific Ocean.

Irrawaddy dolphins swim in pods, or groups, of 3 to 10 dolphins. These dolphins are listed as vulnerable to becoming **extinct**. The main threats they face are getting caught in fishing nets, getting hit by boats, habitat loss, and pollution.

INDO-PACIFIC HUMPBACKED DOLPHIN

The Indo-Pacific humpbacked dolphin lives in the shallow coastal waters of the Indian Ocean and the Pacific Ocean. These dolphins range from the east coast of Africa to Southeast Asia and Australia.

This dolphin's color varies based on its age and in which part of its range it lives. Calves, or babies, are dark gray. They become lighter gray, and pinkish spots appear as they grow into young adult dolphins. In the waters around China and Southeast Asia, adults are white or pinkish white. For this reason, these dolphins are sometimes called Chinese white dolphins.

This drawing shows a side view of an Indo-Pacific humpbacked dolphin.

Indo-Pacific humpbacked dolphins are known to enter rivers, estuaries, and mangrove swamps as they hunt for fish.

DUGONG

The dugong is a large marine mammal that eats underwater grasses. Its large size and diet have helped earn it the nickname sea cow. It lives in warm, shallow coastal waters from east Africa to Australia. Dugongs can stay underwater for up to 6 minutes at a time. They hold themselves upright with their tails and push their heads above water to breathe.

◀ Some believe that dugongs were the animal behind ancient tales of mermaids and sirens.

Dugongs grow to be 13 feet (4 m) long. They can weigh up to 882 pounds (400 kg). ▲

Dugongs have long been hunted for their meat, skin, bones, and teeth. They are also threatened by pollution, getting hit by boats, and getting caught in fishing nets. There are places where they are protected, especially off the coast of Australia. The spread of such protections throughout the rest of its range may help the numbers of this Asian animal recover.

Here a dugong mother and calf swim together. ▼

LAKE BAIKAL SEAL

Lake Baikal seals are the only seal that lives only in freshwater. They are named for the lake in Siberia, in Russia, where they are found. These thickly furred seals live on the ice that covers the lake for several months of the year. They claw holes in the ice so they can dive for fish. In the summer,

Baikal seals regularly stay underwater for 20 minutes but can stay under for as long as 70 minutes.

▲ Winters in Siberia are so cold that huge Lake Baikal freezes over. The seals hunt for fish beneath the ice.

▲ Lake Baikal is the oldest lake in the world. It is 25 million years old. It also is home to about 1,340 animal species. Half of them are not found anywhere else in the world.

Lake Baikal seals molt, or shed their winter coats. Then they move to the rocks along the shore until the ice forms again.

Baikal seals come together mainly to breed. Otherwise they live alone and spend much of their time hunting a fish called golomyanka.

FINLESS PORPOISE

The finless porpoise lives in coastal waters from the Persian Gulf in the west to Japan in the east. It also lives in freshwater in rivers such as the Yangtze River, in China. The finless porpoise gets its name from its lack of a **dorsal fin**. This is the fin that

Finless porpoises have ridges along their backs instead of fins. They swim in both salt water and freshwater.

other porpoises have on their backs.

Like many dolphins and porpoises, the finless porpoise's main **predators** are sharks. The finless porpoise is listed as vulnerable due to several threats from humans, including getting tangled in fishing nets and getting hit by boats.

The finless porpoise has special neck bones that let it move its head freely. This is helpful while trying to catch fish in murky, narrow rivers.

21

MARINE MAMMALS IN DANGER

Many of Asia's marine and freshwater mammals are vulnerable or endangered. China's Yangtze River dolphin is listed as critically endangered but is thought to be extinct. That means this freshwater dolphin is likely gone forever.

People are working to protect Asia's marine mammals. People around the world join groups that ask for laws to protect Earth's oceans and to limit the threats these animals face from human activities. Scientists study marine mammals to learn more about these animals. These efforts could help keep Asia's marine mammals safe.

The Yangtze River dolphin is also called the baiji. None of these dolphins have been seen since 2002. ▼

GLOSSARY

ADAPTATIONS (a-dap-TAY-shunz) Changes in animals that help them live.

BIOME (BY-ohm) A kind of place with certain weather patterns and kinds of plants.

BRACKISH (BRA-kish) Somewhat salty.

DORSAL FIN (DOR-sul FIN) A fin on the back of a fish or water mammal.

ECHOLOCATION (eh-koh-loh-KAY-shun) A method of finding objects by producing a sound and judging the time it takes the echo to return and the direction from which it returns.

ENDANGERED (in-DAYN-jerd) In danger of no longer existing.

ESTUARIES (ES-choo-wer-eez) Areas of water where ocean tides meet rivers.

EXTINCT (ik-STINGKT) No longer existing.

MARINE (muh-REEN) Having to do with the sea.

NURSE (NURS) When a female feeds her baby milk from her body.

PREDATORS (PREH-duh-terz) Animals that kill other animals for food.

SPECIES (SPEE-sheez) One kind of living thing.

VULNERABLE (VUL-neh-reh-bul) Open to being hurt or becoming extinct.

INDEX

B
bodies, 6, 9

D
dugong(s), 6–7, 9, 16–17

E
estuaries, 8, 13

F
fish, 6, 11, 18–19

H
hair(s), 7

L
laws, 9, 22

M
milk, 6

N
nets, 5, 8, 13, 17, 21
numbers, 5, 17

O
oceans, 4, 8–10, 13–14, 22

P
pollution, 5, 8, 13, 17
predators, 21

S
seal(s), 6–7, 9, 18–19
skin, 7, 17
species, 10

WEBSITES

Due to the changing nature of Internet links, PowerKids Press has developed an online list of websites related to the subject of this book. This site is updated regularly. Please use this link to access the list: www.powerkidslinks.com/aoa/dolph/